THE BOSTON MARATHON BOMBING

Running for Their Lives

BY BLAKE HOENA

Consultant:
Richard Bell, PhD
Associate Professor of History
University of Maryland, College Park

CAPSTONE PRESS
a capstone imprint

Tangled History is published by Capstone Press,
1710 Roe Crest Drive, North Mankato, Minnesota 56003
www.mycapstone.com

Library of Congress Cataloging-in-Publication Data is available on the Library of
Congress website

978-1-5435-4196-0 (library binding)
978-1-5435-4200-4 (paperback)
978-1-5435-4204-2 (eBook pdf)

Editorial Credits
Michelle Bisson, editor; Tracy McCabe, designer; Svetlana Zhurkin, media
researcher; Laura Manthe, production specialist

Photo Credits
AP Photo: Charles Krupa, 32; Federal Bureau of Investigations: 24, 26, 42; Getty
Images: Boston Globe, 28, 39, Kevin Morris, 10, Natasha Moustache, 77, New
York Daily News Archive, 47, Stan Honda, 78; Newscom: Cal Sport Media/
Anthony Nesmith, 52, Polaris, 96, Reuters, 64, Reuters/Dominick Reuter, 4,
6, Reuters/Jane Rosenberg, 99, Reuters/Jessica Rinaldi, 45, 55, 101, Reuters/
Kevin Lamarque, 50, Reuters/Lucas Jackson, 84, Reuters/Shannon Stapleton, 61,
Splash News, 35, 103, Splash News/Cambridge Police, 8, UPI/Matt Healey, 88,
USA Today Sports/Winslow Townson, 20, ZUMA Press/Angela Sciaraffa, 17,
ZUMA Press/Boston Police Department, 73, ZUMA Press/Jeremiah Robinson,
92, ZUMA Press/Kenneth Martin, 76, 83, ZUMA Press/VKontakt, 66; Reuters:
Dan Lampariello, cover

Printed and bound in the United States of America.
PA49

TABLE OF CONTENTS

Foreword...4
1) Getting Ready for the Race.........................8
2) Explosions Rock Boylston Street 20
3) C for Critical 32
4) No Love in the City 42
5) Nails and Ball Bearings.................................... 52
6) Working Around the Clock 66
7) Shootout on Laurel Street................................ 78
8) Identify and Capture 84

Epilogue 98
Timeline.. 106
Glossary 108
Critical Thinking Questions............................... 109
Internet Sites 109
Further Reading.. 110
Selected Bibliography 111
Index... 112
About the Author 112

The first wave of Boston Marathon runners set off hoping to make good time in the race.

FOREWORD

On April 19, 1897, John McDermott won the first ever Boston Marathon. He was one of only 15 participants that year and completed the course in just under three hours. Since then the

Boston Marathon has taken place every year, making it the longest continuously run marathon in the world. It is held on the third Monday in April. This day is known as Patriot's Day, a holiday that commemorates the Battles of Lexington and Concord. Fought near Boston, these were the first battles of the American Revolutionary War.

The Boston Marathon has also grown into one of the largest races worldwide. More than 30,000 people participate each year. Runners come from every state and nearly 100 countries. Half a million spectators gather to watch the race. Thousands more people work in support of the event. Volunteers operate refreshment stations, medical staff oversee emergency care, and police officers patrol the route.

To runners and event organizers, the 117th running of the Boston Marathon started like any other Marathon Monday.

Runners leaving Hopkinton, Massachusetts, had no idea of what would await them in Boston later that day.

The morning of April 15, 2013, runners gathered in Hopkinton, Massachusetts, just west of Boston. A sign outside of town read, "It All Starts Here!" Hopkinton has been the official starting point of the Boston Marathon since 1924.

The mood was festive. It felt more like a big celebration than an athletic event. Music blared while racers chatted excitedly. They were all smiles as they grabbed refreshments and stretched out. The biggest concern for most of the participants was simply making it across the finish line 26.2 miles away.

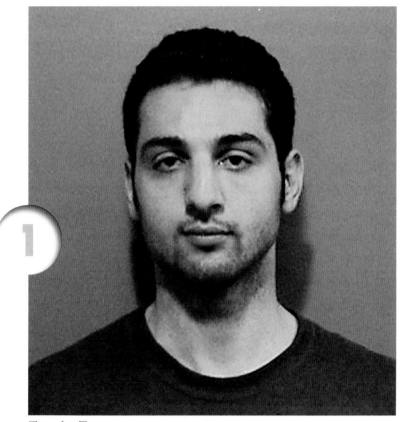
Tamerlan Tsarnaev

GETTING READY FOR THE RACE

The night before the 117th running of the Boston Marathon, Tamerlan Tsarnaev was at home with his younger brother, Dzhokhar. They chatted as they prepared for the next day's race. Often their conversations were about politics and events back home in Kyrgyzstan.

As Tamerlan and Dzhokhar worked, they stood over two pressure cookers. Often such pots are used to make soups and stews. They are airtight, and when their contents are heated, the steam trapped inside them can create intense pressure and temperatures. But Tamerlan had another purpose—something other than cooking—in mind for them. He showed his younger brother how to pack them with gunpowder, nails and ball bearings, and Vaseline.

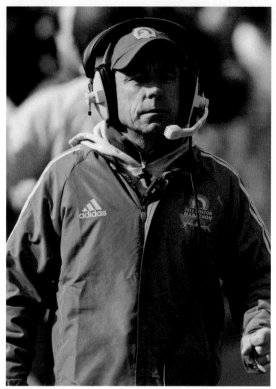

David McGillivray felt confident that all was as it should be at the start of the 2013 Boston Marathon.

David McGillivray

Main Street, Hopkinton, Massachusetts
Monday, April 15, 2013, 6:00 a.m.

David McGillivray woke up before sunrise. He had a quick bite to eat and then laced up his running shoes. This had long been a part of his ritual on Marathon Mondays. For the past 25 years, he had served as race director of the Boston Marathon. An avid runner, he had completed more than 100 marathons, including a streak of 40 Boston Marathons in a row. He was familiar with what it took to organize a successful race.

By 6:00 a.m. McGillivray was in Hopkinton. He entered Athletes' Village, a staging area set up on the grounds of the local high school. The runners would gather here before the race. McGillivray quickly inspected everything, from the check-in stations to the portable restrooms. When he was satisfied, he headed down to the starting line to make sure everything there was ready as well.

At all times, a volunteer with a handheld radio was close behind him. McGillivray would rely on this person to help him stay in touch with his many assistants along the course. He was managing a huge event that needed thousands of helpers. The marathon had taken months to organize. It ran through eight communities from Hopkinton to Boston. Streets had been blocked off to keep cars from the route. Fencing and cement barriers were set up to separate spectators from the runners. Along the course, dozens of emergency and refreshment stations had been set up and needed to be attended.

One of the biggest issues McGillivray had worked out over his years as director was the timing of when racers start. It would not be a successful race if top runners had to fight through a crowd of slower racers. Runners would be released in organized waves. At 9:00 a.m. the mobility-impaired division would start off the race. Some people in this group needed extra time to finish, but it was a small group. Next would come the wheelchair divisions, followed by the Handcycle divisions.

McGillivray knew that once those racers were well on their way, the runners in the elite divisions could step onto the course. It would be mostly empty, and they would not have to worry about interference from other racers. The elite women would start at 9:32 a.m. and the elite men at 10:00 a.m. Shortly after that, everyone else would be released in three large waves with thousands of runners each.

On average, runners finished the Boston Marathon in just under four hours. That meant between 2:00 p.m. and 3:00 p.m. would be the busiest period at the finish line. Friends and families of runners would be gathered up and down Boylston Street where the race ended. Runners would be picking up personal items stored at the end of the race. McGillivray knew this would be a chaotic point in the event.

Before heading on to other duties, McGillivray made sure that the race marshals were ready with the starting schedule. He hoped to keep ahead of any potential problems.

Natalie Stavas

Main Street, Hopkinton, Massachusetts
Monday, April 15, 2013, morning

Dr. Natalie Stavas worked as a physician at Boston Children's Hospital. She was excited to be taking part in her fifth Boston Marathon despite a recent injury. Weeks earlier she had fractured a bone in one of her feet. On top of that she was exhausted from putting in long hours at work. But running in the marathon was a goal she had trained hard to achieve. She was not going to let anything stop her. Also, she did not want to disappoint her father. Joseph Stavas had traveled from Chapel Hill, North Carolina, to run the marathon with her.

Like thousands of other runners, the pair arrived at Hopkinton well before the official start of the race. They hopped off a shuttle bus and strolled toward the gates of Athletes' Village. Their white bibs, which meant they'd run with the second wave, were already pinned to their shirts.

As Stavas and her father wandered through Athletes' Village, a blue sky stretched out above them. It was a beautiful spring day. Perfect for running the race to Boston.

The pair walked past refreshment stands offering coffee and sports drinks. Snack stands had energy bars and fruit for the runners. It was incredible to be surrounded by so many like-minded people. There were thousands of marathon enthusiasts from around the world.

It was a celebratory atmosphere, heightened by the fact that not just anyone could run this race.

Boston Marathon runners had to earn entry. For the women's 18–34 age group, Stavas had qualified by besting a time of 3 hours, 35 minutes, at another marathon. For the men's 55–59 age group, her father had qualified by beating a time of 3 hours, 40 minutes. Neither were easy feats. They knew they were among an exclusive group of marathoners.

As the time ticked closer to 9:00 a.m. the buzz of excitement intensified. Racers began to leave the village and head down Grove Street toward the starting line. Fans were crowding around and ready to cheer on each group of racers as they set off. Several divisions of runners would head out before the first wave of general public runners, who wore red bibs, would leave—just after 10:00 a.m. As Natalie and her father waited for their start time, they bounced from one foot to the other to keep their muscles loose. At 10:20 a.m. the runners in wave two lunged forward. Stavas and her father were all smiles as they set off.

The race started on Hopkinton's East Main Street and headed east. The first few miles were a gentle, downward slope. Stavas and her father set off at a steady pace. They reached the 5-kilometer mark in under 30 minutes. Then they wound their way through the small towns of Ashland and Framingham before heading down Central Street in Natick. Along the way, small groups of spectators lined the roads to cheer them on. Stavas knew the biggest crowds would be waiting near the finish line.

Thomas Menino

Brigham and Women's Hospital, Boston, Massachusetts
April 15, 2013, 9:00 a.m.

Thomas Menino, Boston's longest-serving mayor, had been in office since 1993. That was almost 20 years of Marathon Mondays, and he loved them. Boston was on display for the world to see. Its marathon was one of the world's most prestigious races. It made him proud to represent this city.

In previous years, Menino had sat in the front row of the grandstands on Boylston Street. He would watch the elite runners cross the finish line, and then he'd crown the men's winner. But earlier in the month, he had broken a bone in his right leg and

Thomas Menino

injured his ankle. He'd had surgery the Saturday before the race to repair his injuries. This Marathon Monday he was lying on a hospital bed ready to watch the beginning of the race. Governor Deval Patrick would take his place at the finish line.

After years of involvement with the planning of the race, Menino knew that fully securing the 26.2-mile stretch of the Boston Marathon was nearly impossible. It was what is known as a soft target, an area difficult to protect. Menino had worried about this problem for the past 20 years. But there was just too much ground to cover, and too many people either taking part in the race or watching. At least there had been few issues beyond thefts and rowdy spectators in past runnings of the Boston Marathon.

Still, city and state officials had stepped up security measures since the 9/11 terrorist attacks in 2001. And for 2013, the number of officers out on the streets had even been increased over past years. Along with hundreds of police officers in Boston alone, Massachusetts National Guard members were also brought in to help.

Other security measures had been taken. Nearly 1,000 uniformed officers mingled with the crowd, keeping an eye out for any suspicious activity. Helicopters whirled overhead to monitor the event. Several K-9 units with bomb-sniffing dogs were also on hand. They would continually sweep areas around the finish line. Menino's own son, Detective Thomas Menino Jr., was stationed near the finish line.

With all these measures in place, Menino felt that the race was in good hands. He was confident that this year's Boston Marathon would be another successful event for his city.

Smoke filled the air at the finish line of the 117th Boston Marathon after two bombs went off. People ran in confusion and fear.

EXPLOSIONS ROCK BOYLSTON STREET

William Evans

It was not unusual for Boston Police Superintendent William Evans to be off duty on Marathon Monday. The 117th running of the race was his 18th Boston Marathon as a racer.

Today, he had been grouped with wave two, and he quickly found his stride, setting off at a pace just under 8 minutes per mile. While that was far slower than the elite runners, who ran about 5-minute miles, Evan's was running a strong race for someone in his mid-50s.

Evans reached the halfway mark in Wellesley at 1 hour, 45 minutes. He had slowed to just over 8 minutes per mile, but he was still having a solid race. He was on pace to finish in about 3 hours, 30 minutes, which would match his time last year.

From there, he ran northeast up Washington Street. At the Newton Fire Station, he turned east onto Commonwealth Avenue and then headed toward the most difficult section of the course. Until this point, much of the race had been run slightly downhill, but that changed at mile 16. In front of him there was a series of four hills, with the last one dubbed Heartbreak Hill, coming just after mile 20. Evans knew that it wasn't the climb that did runners in. The hill was a mere 91 feet. But being toward the end of the race, when runners were hitting their wall, the hill forced many to falter.

Evans's legs were feeling numb. His breaths were more labored than when he had set off. But he had done this 17 times before. So he leaned into Heartbreak Hill and ran up, with his pace slowing only a little.

From there, the last few miles were a steady descent. Evans was even able to pick up his pace a bit. Heading into the final mile of the race, he recalled a saying common among runners in the Boston Marathon. Right on Hereford Street and then left on Boylston Street. After those turns there was only half a mile left in the race. As he ran that last section, Evans saw the blue uniforms of Boston police officers lining the course. Being cheered on by his fellow members of the police force made him feel a twinge of pride. Along with them, thousands of spectators stood on the other side of the barricades blocking off the street. They cheered and hollered as every runner crossed the finish line. Then Evans was across in a time of 3 hours, 34 minutes.

Tamerlan Tsarnaev

Norfolk Street, Cambridge, Massachusetts
Monday, April 15, 2013, afternoon

Tamerlan and his brother left the house in Cambridge after the runners in the Boston Marathon had set off. Tamerlan wore a black baseball cap and dark sunglasses. Dzhokhar wore his white baseball cap backwards and also had on a dark jacket. Both brothers carried heavy backpacks slung across their backs. Like thousands of other people in the area, they headed out to find a spot along the Boston Marathon's route near the finish line. To them, the finish line was the right spot for what they'd planned to do.

Dzhokhar Tsarnaev (left) and his brother, Tamerlan, walked into the crowd watching the Boston Marathon as though they were also mere spectators.

The journey to this point in Tamerlan's life had been a long one. Of Chechen descent, he had been born in Russia but grew up in Kyrgyzstan, where his brother, Dzhokhar, was born. In 2003, when he was 16, Tamerlan moved to the United States to join his family in Massachusetts. For some time he had hoped to become a naturalized citizen like Dzhokhar. He even got married to an American, Katherine Russell, and they had a daughter, Zahara. But he became disillusioned by the American way of life and its politics. He particularly hated how he felt the U.S.

government persecuted Muslims. And he still had strong ties to Chechnya. For years, rebels there had been fighting for independence from Russia. Many people called the rebels terrorists or extremists, but Tamerlan felt that their cause was just, even if they committed horrific acts of violence. He felt the same about his and his brother's mission. And now was the time to carry it out.

Dzhokhar Tsarnaev

Norfolk Street, Cambridge, Massachusetts
Monday, April 15, 2013, 2:37 p.m.

Hours after the first runners crossed the finish line, Dzhokhar was with his brother on Boylston Street. Tamerlan was a big influence on his younger brother, and Dzhokhar often followed his lead.

As they walked behind the crowd lining the street, he was a few steps behind Tamerlan. The brothers stopped for a moment to watch the runners stream by. Then they split up. Dzhokhar paused in front of the Forum restaurant while Tamerlan continued on down the street.

Dzhokhar kept looking impatiently at his phone.

Dzhokhar was later identified as a suspect by his backpack and white cap.

After a few minutes, he called his brother. Once they were done talking, he stepped toward the street. He slipped his backpack from his shoulder and set it on the ground. Then he hurriedly walked away.

Jeff Bauman

Boylston Street, Boston, Massachusetts
Monday, April 15, 2013, 2:48 p.m.

Jeff Bauman stood near the finish line in front of Marathon Sports. He had arrived with a couple of friends about half an hour earlier. He was there to cheer on his girlfriend, Erin Hurley. The sidewalks were packed rows deep with spectators. But he and his friends found a spot where he hoped he could see Erin cross the finish line.

One man oddly stood out to Bauman. He was wearing dark sunglasses and a dark baseball cap. A backpack was slung across his back. While everyone around Bauman was cheering and clapping as runners crossed the finish line, this man was not. He stood alone and looked at his phone.

Bauman turned back to watch for Erin. He wondered where she was. She should be here by now.

Suddenly, a loud bang rocked the area and a plume of white smoke filled the air. The explosion threw Bauman to the ground. Everything that happened next was a chaotic blur.

Police Superintendent William Evans at a Boston Marathon event

Natalie Stavas

Boylston Street, Boston, Massachusetts
Monday, April 15, 2013, 2:49 p.m.

Despite her sore foot, Stavas was having an enjoyable run with her father. They had hit the halfway mark in less than two hours. They were

running a solid pace of 9 minutes, 30 seconds per mile. Her foot forced her to run more slowly than she normally would. Still, the pair were on their way to finishing the grueling event in just over four hours.

Leading up to the finish line, police officers in yellow vests stood along the course. Flags for various nations also lined the road. Spectators clapped and cheered the runners on to the finish line. She heard a loud booming noise near the finish line. Like everyone around her, Stavas scanned the area to figure out what had made that sound. She wondered if it had been fireworks or maybe a cannon. There was typically a celebratory atmosphere around the finish line.

Then another explosion boomed closer than the first one. When spectators started running her way, Stavas knew something was wrong.

In the panic, people screamed, "Gunman!" "Sniper!" "Bomber!"

Chaos surrounded her, and at that moment she realized she had to make a choice. She could join those fleeing the scene. Or she could run toward the commotion—toward where people might be injured, or worse.

Her medical training took over. After running nearly 26 miles and with a foot that was causing her pain with every step, Stavas rushed forward. She ran through the crowd and toward the plume of smoke in front of the Forum restaurant. A police officer tried to stop her, but she shouted, "I'm a pediatric physician! I'm a pediatric physician." She kept running.

What she saw horrified her. It was worse than any trauma she had seen at the hospital where she worked. Metal barricades had been knocked over. People were lying on the pavement. There was lots of blood. People were shouting as they ran away. The injured lay on the ground moaning and crying in pain. Some were clutching the bloody stumps where parts of a limbs had been blown off.

Stavas leaped into action. She performed CPR on a young woman until paramedics arrived. Stavas did not know whether the woman would survive, but she didn't have time to think about that. Dozens more were badly injured, and they might lose their lives right here on the street. She used a torn piece of clothing to stop the bleeding from one woman's wounds. She helped a man whose foot had been injured. Then she helped another person with a leg injury. Stavas continued until a police officer pulled her away.

"This area needs to be secured. It's not safe," she was told. "There might be another bomb."

After Jeff Bauman was injured, emergency workers and volunteers rushed to the rescue.

C FOR CRITICAL

Jeff Bauman

Jeff Bauman saw smoke in front of him. It took him a moment to realize that he was lying on the ground. He looked around to see what had happened. People were frantically scattering in all directions. Some screamed while fleeing in panic. Others, injured, cried out in pain. Bauman looked around for his friends. One of them was lying on the ground a few feet away. She was hurt but alive.

Blood was everywhere. There was also a terrible burning smell, like cooked meat, in the air. Then Bauman glanced down at his legs. From the knees down, all he saw was a bloody mess of blackened flesh and bone.

Another explosion shook the area. Bauman felt as if he were in a war zone. He had no idea if he was going to live or die.

But through the chaos, a man rushed in to help.

"Get shirts! Shoelaces! Anything!" the man yelled out. "People are bleeding."

Then, with a finger dipped in blood, he wrote C on Bauman's head. C for critical. Moments later, a man in a cowboy hat lifted Bauman into a wheelchair. He was rushed to a waiting ambulance, which sped off to Boston Medical Center.

Carlos Arredondo

Boylston Street, Boston, Massachusetts
Monday, April 15, 2013, afternoon

Carlos Arredondo, wearing a white cowboy hat, was across the street near Marathon Sports when the first bomb went off. He was there as a spectator, but he had received disaster training from the Red Cross. He leaped over the barricade in front of him and ran into the smoke-filled bomb zone. He started to pull toppled fencing out of the way so that emergency workers could get through to the injured.

Arredondo was horrified by what he saw.

Carlos Arredondo's quick thinking helped save the life of Jeff Bauman at the marathon. He and his wife stood together at their home a few days later.

Blood had been splattered across the area. There were severed limbs on the ground. People were bleeding. Then he saw a man with legs that ended in bloody hunks of flesh just below the knees. He was struggling to sit up. Arredondo ran over to help him.

"My name's Carlos," he said. "You're going to be okay."

Glancing around, Arredondo saw a sweater lying on the ground. He ripped it into strips and used them as tourniquets, tying them around the ends of the man's legs to staunch the bleeding.

An emergency worker was pushing an empty wheelchair. Arredondo grabbed it, picked up the injured man, and set him in the wheelchair. Then he began pushing him away from scene. A woman stepped in to help him push the wheelchair. A police officer jumped in front of them to clear the way. They reached an ambulance and lifted the man into it.

"You're going to be okay," Arredondo assured the man as the ambulance doors slammed shut.

David McGillivray

Another part of David McGillivray's Marathon Monday ritual was running the course after everyone else had set off. He had done it every year he had served as director. After the elite runners had crossed the finished line, he changed into running clothes and headed back to Hopkinton. He arrived just before 3:00 p.m. He went to the starting line and began to stretch. State troopers on motorcycles were on standby to escort him. He had only been there a few minutes when a friend called him over. The friend had just received a call from his daughter, and told McGillivray, "a bomb went off at the finish."

McGillivray was shocked. He immediately worried not only about the runners and spectators, but also about his family. His wife would be waiting for him near the finish line. He knew he had to get back to Boston. His friend asked the state troopers to take them there. The troopers agreed and they all sped off.

They arrived in Boston to find that emergency medical tents had already been set up. The injured were receiving the care they needed. McGillivray knew that he would only be in the way if he tried to help. So he set off to do what he had done for the past 25 years—see to the people running the race. Thousands of runners had not crossed the finish line. Many were from out of town and would need to get back to their hotels. They must be scared and exhausted, he thought. They probably had not been able to contact friends or family. Their phones, wallets, and other personal items had been stored in plastic yellow bags at the end of the race. McGillivray set to work organizing them in hopes of finding their owners.

William Evans

Boylston Street, Boston, Massachusetts
Monday, April 15, 2013, afternoon

After finishing his 18th Boston Marathon, William Evans headed over to the Boston Athletic Club a few miles away. He was there when he heard the news that two bombs had exploded near the

Emergency workers rushed to the scene of the explosions.

finish line. He hurried home, put on his uniform, and then raced back to Boylston Street.

Evans stepped into the role of the Boston Police's point person on the streets. With Police Commissioner Edward Davis, he designed a plan of action. He was in charge of making sure the plan was implemented. He and Davis knew that one of the first priorities was to ensure there were no more bombs. Evans had bomb-sniffing dogs sweep the area. He ordered his officers to set up a perimeter with a 20-block radius around the finish line. That would keep people safely away.

Thomas Menino

Brigham and Women's Hospital, Boston, Massachusetts
Monday, April 15, 2013, afternoon

Mayor Thomas Menino had kept a close eye on the race, wanting to learn who won. The fastest time had been logged by Tom Davis of the United States in the Handcycle division. His time was 1:17:59. Rita Jeptoo of Kenya was the top women's finisher, with a time of 2:26:25. Lelisa Desisa of Ethiopia led the male runners, clocking in at 2:10:22.

Menino had been resting in his hospital bed when a police officer barged into his room. "Mayor, we've just had an explosion at the marathon. Not one, but two," he said.

Despite his doctor's protests, Menino quickly prepared to check out of the hospital. As the mayor of Boston, he was not going to sit around while his city was in trouble. He needed to be out in public and supporting those reeling from the disaster.

"Get me some clothes and a wheelchair," he told one of his staff.

Menino headed to Copley Square, a public area in the heart of Boston just east of the finishing line. There, police had set up a command center. Menino was in a great deal of pain. He gritted his teeth as his sore leg shook. He wasn't able to get out of the vehicle that had driven him to the square. So he sat and listened to a police scanner and did what he could to help direct emergency efforts.

4

Tamerlan Tsarnaev became known as "Black Hat" to those seeking the terrorist. But right after the bombing, no one had yet made the connection.

NO LOVE IN THE CITY

Tamerlan and Dzhokhar Tsarnaev

Cambridge, Massachusetts
Monday, April 15, 2013, 3:14 p.m.

After setting off two bombs, Tamerlan and his brother left Boylston Street. They headed back to Cambridge. On the way they made one quick stop.

Tamerlan parked and waited in the car while Dzhokhar ran inside a grocery store not far from Tamerlan's house. A few minutes later, he came back with a half gallon of milk. He hopped into the car, and they drove off.

About 40 minutes after the bombing, Tamerlan received a text. A friend wanted to swing by to pick up Tamerlan and take him out for dinner. Dzhokhar joined them. The trio headed over to Man-O-Salwa Kabob & Grill on Summer Street in Somerville.

They laughed and joked at dinner. They also talked about the horrific events of the bombing.

Later, Tamerlan went home. He stayed there with his wife and daughter for the next couple of days.

Richard DesLauriers

FBI Command Post, Boston, Massachusetts
Monday, April 15, 2013, afternoon

Shortly after the bombings, Richard DesLauriers attended a meeting with the heads of city and state law enforcement agencies. Massachusetts governor Deval Patrick also attended. DesLauriers was the special agent in charge of the Boston division of the FBI. Patrick and the group determined that the FBI should take the lead in the investigation.

DesLauriers had many questions. First, he needed to know who set off the bombs. Typically, when a terrorist group attacked, they claimed responsibility. So far, no one had done so. He also needed to know if there were other bombs. He knew the area needed to be secured. Once that happened, his team could feel safe focusing on evidence gathering. Finally there was the question of what to do with all the evidence that would be gathered.

Richard DesLauriers

In bomb explosion investigations, DesLauriers knew
that forensic teams had to search for even the tiniest
pieces of the bombs. All the evidence would be sorted
through at a large warehouse near the airport. He
immediately brought in hundreds of FBI agents to
help collect evidence. Agents were dispatched to
interview people at the hospital. Others headed down
to the bomb sites.

DesLauriers also knew there would be lots of visual evidence. The Boston Marathon was televised by both national and international media organizations. Businesses in the bombing area had surveillance cameras. There were also thousands of spectators who had been taking videos and pictures. DesLauriers sent out agents to start gathering as much of this visual evidence as possible.

Cheryl Fiandaca

Northshore Mall, Boston, Massachusetts
Monday, April 15, 2013, 3:39 p.m.

While out shopping at the mall with her teenage niece, Cheryl Fiandaca received a call from Commissioner Davis about the bombings.

"We need to push this out and let people know what's happening," he said.

Fiandaca was bureau chief of public information for the Boston Police Department. She was in charge of all its social media. She also knew how easily rumors can spread under chaotic situations like what just happened down on Boylston Street.

Cheryl Fiandaca

47

She wanted to provide people with an official source of information. Almost an hour after the bombs exploded on Boylston Street, she tweeted, "Boston Police confirming explosion at marathon finish line with injuries." #tweetfromthebeat via @CherylFiandaca

Fiandaca left the mall with her niece in tow. She needed to get back to her department's command center so she could oversee the communications it sent out. She got into her car and handed her niece her phone. As Fiandaca drove away, she told her niece what to tweet.

"Updates to follow. Please clear area around marathon finish line" #tweetfromthebeat via @CherylFiandaca

Dzhokhar Tsarnaev

Twitter
Monday, April 15, 2013, 5:04 p.m.

It had been only a few hours since Dzhokhar had helped set off the explosions on Boylston Street. News outlets were reporting that three people had been killed and more than 250 others had been injured. Dzhokhar logged onto his Twitter account. He posted a tweet that read, *"Ain't no love in the heart of the city, stay safe people."*

Barack Obama

Not long after the bombing, President Barack Obama received a call from FBI director Robert Mueller. With multiple bombs going off, Mueller told the president that it was likely an act of terrorism. Obama knew the country would be reeling after such news. He needed to respond quickly to console everyone and let them know that the government was on top of the situation. He appeared on TV to do so at 6:10 p.m.

"I've directed the full resources of the federal government to help state and local authorities protect our people, increase security around the United States as necessary, and investigate what happened," Obama said.

Obama mentioned that he had been in touch with both Governor Patrick and Mayor Menino.

President Barack Obama tried to reassure the nation that the terrorists who set off bombs at the Boston Marathon would be found and held responsible.

He spoke of the heroics of the first responders. He shared his sympathy with those who had been hurt in the bombings, and with their families.

"We still do not know who did this or why," he continued. "And people shouldn't jump to conclusions before we have all the facts. But make no mistake—we will get to the bottom of this. And we will find out who did this; we'll find out why they did this. Any responsible individuals, any responsible groups will feel the full weight of justice."

Richard DesLauriers (center) and other officials did their best to keep the public informed about the search for the terrorists.

NAILS
AND BALL
BEARINGS

Richard DesLauriers

FBI Command Post, Boston, Massachusetts
Tuesday, April 16, 2013, morning

As soon as the injured were cleared from the bomb area, Richard DesLauriers had a forensics team start scouring the area for evidence. They worked around the clock, walking shoulder to shoulder in white jumpsuits over an area to look for any possible clues. Anything that looked out of the ordinary might turn out to be important. The jumpsuits protected them from hazardous materials and kept them from contaminating the crime scene.

DesLauriers knew that one key step to finding out who the bombers were was finding out the type of explosive device they used. Also, this could help the team determine whether there was a threat of further bombs. Many people in the FBI and in local law enforcement worried that other bombs might be set off.

DesLauriers had his forensics team gather every piece of shrapnel from the bomb. They collected bent nails. Ball bearings were picked out of pools of drying blood. Such pieces of shrapnel had ripped through the crowd, embedding themselves in bystanders and severing limbs. Everything was photographed, bagged, and tagged to be taken back to the warehouse. Investigators noted that some of the ball bearings were held together by petroleum jelly.

Deval Patrick, Thomas Menino, and Richard DesLauriers

Westin Hotel, Boston, Massachusetts
Tuesday, April 16, 2013, morning

On Tuesday morning, local officials held a press conference to reassure the public of the progress in the investigation. Governor Deval Patrick spoke first.

"Thanks for coming this morning," he said.

At a press conference the day after the bombings, Governor Deval Patrick (left) explained that the bombs used at the marathon had been found.

". . . Two devices were found yesterday. All of the other parcels have beend examined, but there are no unexploded bombs. There were no other explosive devices found . . ."

Then Mayor Thomas Menino spoke. He was still in a wheelchair from his surgery just days earlier.

He wanted to commend those who stepped in to help during the tragedy. "We know our heroes," he stated. "They are the men and women who wear helmets, the badges. The runners who helped us during this time of need." He added, "Boston is a strong city. We are a city that will get through this."

Menino helped popularize the "Boston Strong" slogan. This meant that Bostonians remained strong and committed to helping each other recover even during a difficult time.

Then, Richard DesLauriers stepped up to the podium. He echoed the words of Patrick and Menino. He complimented local medical staff and law enforncement. He also said, "there are no additional threats." DesLauriers ended by saying that his team was just starting to process all the evidence that had been gathered from the crime scene.

Dzhokhar Tsarnaev

Junior Auto Body, Somerville, Massachusetts
Tuesday, April 16, 2013, 12:00 p.m.

About midday, Dzhokhar headed over to Junior Auto Body Shop in Somerville. The shop was not far from Tamerlan's house in Cambridge. Dzhokhar had dropped off a white Mercedes Benz two weeks earlier. He had said it was his girlfriend's car, and the rear bumper had been damaged.

At the shop, Dzhokhar spoke to owner Gilberto Tercetti. Tercetti told him that the car was not ready.

Dzhokhar seemed nervous and bit his nails.

"I need it now," he said.

Tercetti gave him the keys, and Dzhokhar drove off without waiting for the car to be repaired. After driving around for a little while, he headed back to his brother's house. Later that afternoon Azamat Tazhayakov stopped by the house. The friends hopped into Dzhokhar's green Honda Civic and headed over to Azamat's apartment in New Bedford. For hours, Dzhokhar and Azamat played video games. At one point, Dzhokhar took a short break to Skype with Tamerlan in private.

Jeff Bauman

Boston Medical Center, Boston, Massachusetts
Tuesday, April 16, 2013, afternoon

Friends and family were in his hospital room when Bauman awoke from surgery. He felt heavily sedated but agitated. He had something to say. But he was weak and struggled to speak. He motioned for a pen and paper, and then he began to write. He tried to write about the guy he had seen with the backpack. He believed it was the bomber.

Soon FBI agents were at Bauman's bedside. He described the man as someone with dark glasses, a baseball cap, and a backpack. When asked why he noticed the man, Bauman replied that it was because, "He was all business." He explained that the man seemed to be there for a reason other than to cheer on the runners.

Over the next day, FBI agents had Bauman go through stacks and stacks of photographs. He was exhausted but pushed himself. He needed to help. But he did not spot the man he had seen in any of the photos.

Richard DesLauriers

Westin Hotel, Boston, Massachusetts
Tuesday, April 16, 2013, afternoon

Late Tuesday afternoon, Special Agent Richard DesLauriers stepped up to the podium at a news conference. He knew the public wanted to know what was happening with the investigation. He needed to let people know that progress was being made and the FBI was in control of the situation. There had already been false reports about suspects being detained.

Fear and misinformation could not only hamper his investigation but also make it less likely that the public would help. And his team needed all the help they could get to find out who had set off the bombs.

"Let me recap our efforts in this investigation," he started. "The first step law enforcement took was to secure the physical area around the blast for the purpose of preserving evidence in the area related to the devices itself. . . ." DesLauriers went on to describe the forensic evidence recovery efforts at the blast site. All the evidence recovered, after being sorted through at the warehouse, was sent to the FBI's Laboratory in Quantico, Virginia. There, examiners reconstructed the device. The nails and ball bearings they found made them think it was a pressure cooker bomb. DesLauriers also noted that among the items found were pieces of black nylon, which could be from a backpack.

Along with this information, he put out a request to the public for cooperation, and asked them to share any information, photos, or video recordings they might have. "We ask that businesses review and preserve surveillance video and other business records in their original form." Most of the businesses near the bombing sites had security cameras. Newspaper crews were filming near the finish line. On top of that, thousands of spectators with smart phones were on hand on Boylston Street.

Kevin Swindon

FBI Command Post, Boston, Massachusetts
Tuesday, April 16, 2013, afternoon

Special Agent Kevin Swindon was in charge of the FBI's Computer Analysis Response Team. The team was scouring through all the hours of video footage that had been supplied by spectators and businesses. They looked through thousands upon thousands of images. His team's focus was on surveillance cameras around the two bombing sites. They even had footage from the Forum restaurant. But it did not clearly show where the bomb went off.

But thanks to the call to the public for any images and video of that day, investigators got a lucky break. A man supplied a photo showing the Forum just before the first explosion. In the photo,

Officials gathered evidence and took crime scene photos of the Forum restaurant a day after the bombings. These photos helped investigators in the search to find a suspect.

they spotted Martin Richard, an 8-year-old boy who had died in the bombing. Upon closer inspection, Swindon's team also noticed a black backpack on the ground just feet from where Martin and his family had stood. Swindon believed the suspect was somewhere in that photo.

Again, they looked at the surveillance video. They wanted to see if anyone in it was also in the photo. That would mean the person must have been walking toward the bomb site.

One figure stood out. It was a man wearing a white baseball cap backwards. They even spotted images of him with a backpack over his shoulder. He became known as White Hat. As the team continued to look through more footage from before the bombing, they kept their eyes out for any sign of White Hat.

In the end, they realized they were looking for two bombers. The two bombs had been set off blocks away from each other and just seconds apart, so White Hat had to have had at least one accomplice.

They found a new lead when viewing footage from Whiskey Smokehouse, just down Boylston Street from the Forum. They noticed someone walking in front of White Hat. He had on a black hat and sunglasses and carried a backpack similar to White Hat's. They now had suspect 2, or Black Hat, as he came to be known.

As they looked through more footage and photos, they spotted the two together. Swindon's team became more and more confident that these two were their prime suspects. But they had no idea who they were.

Richard DesLauriers

FBI Command Post, Boston, Massachusetts
Tuesday, April 16, 2013, night

By Tuesday night, DesLauriers's forensics team had found everything they need to reconstruct the bombs that had been used. They had discovered the circuit boards and detonating devices. The bent-up lid to a pressure cooker had also been found on the roof of a nearby hotel. DesLauriers's investigators were then able to discover a store that sold the model of pressure cooker that was used. The team hoped this might provide a lead to who had set off the bombs.

Also, finding the lid and pieces of shrapnel helped them determine the type of bombs used. Viewing video of the white smoke in the explosions

The remains of one of the explosives were found by the crime scene investigation team.

led DesLauriers's team to establish that the devices used gun powder. Nails and ball bearings were packed in a pressure cooker with a detonating device—a pressure cooker bomb. When the gunpowder was ignited, it created a great deal of pressure inside the sealed pressure cooker. That pressure caused it to explode, sending out deadly shrapnel. Knowing the type of bomb used solved one piece of the puzzle.

Dzhokhar Tsarnaev

University of Massachusetts Dartmouth,
North Dartmouth, Massachusetts
Tuesday, April 16, 2013, 9:05 p.m.

Tuesday night Dzhokhar was at his dormitory, Pine Dale Hall, on the University of Massachusetts Dartmouth campus. He had started attending the university back in 2011, and initially majored in marine biology. The night after the bombing, Dzhokhar walked around the dormitory and chatted with fellow students. He tried to appear calm and relaxed, hoping to give everyone the impression that everything was normal. Even his roommate, Andrew Dwinells, didn't seem to think that anything was unusual.

At 9:05 p.m. Dzhokhar went to the fitness center to work out. While he was there, a classmate mentioned the bombing.

"Yeah, tragedies happen like this all the time," Dzhokhar replied. "It's too bad."

Later that night, feeling confident that he was in the clear, Dzhokhar posted a tweet. It read, "I'm a stress free kind of guy."

Azamat Tazhayakov (left) and Dias Kadyrbayev at first had no idea that their friend Dzhokhar (right) was a suspect in the bombings.

WORKING AROUND THE CLOCK

Jeff Bauman

Boston Medical Center, Boston, Massachusetts
Wednesday, April 17, 2013, afternoon

Just two days after Bauman nearly lost his life, an FBI sketch artist walked into his room. Over the next couple of hours, Bauman did his best to describe the suspicious figure he had seen at the marathon. To his surprise, the artist's final result was an incredible likeness of the man he remembered.

Dzhokhar Tsarnaev

University of Massachusetts Dartmouth, North Dartmouth, Massachusetts
Wednesday, April 17, 2013, night till Thursday, April 18, 2013, 4:00 p.m.

On Wednesday, Dzhokhar spent the day going about his usual business. He attended classes. Later, he worked out at the fitness center. He hung out with some fellow soccer players at a restaurant.

And that night, he again headed to New Bedford to play video games with his friend Azamat. He stayed there until about midnight before returning to his dorm room.

Dzhokhar attended classes Thursday afternoon. At one point he received a text from Azamat. His friend needed a ride back to his apartment after finishing up with classes. Dzhokhar met up with Azamat, and then the pair headed to New Bedford.

After dropping off Azamat, Dzhokhar drove off in his green Honda Civic and likely stopped at his dormitory briefly before going to his brother's house in Cambridge.

Richard DesLauriers

Boston, Massachusetts
Thursday, April 18, 2013, 5:20 p.m.

Late Thursday afternoon Richard DesLauriers stepped up to a podium at the Sheraton Hotel in Boston. TV cameras were focused on him. He took a breath, knowing he was about to make a very important announcement.

Since the discovery of the bombing suspects Black Hat and White Hat, a debate had been going on. DesLauriers and other officials in charge of the investigation had been trying to decide whether to release the suspects' images to the public. Some feared that the suspects might flee if they saw their pictures being broadcast. But eventually the need to discover who these two men were outweighed that fear. The pressure was on to capture them before another bomb was set off, so DesLauriers got behind the idea of showing the public images of the two suspects in hopes someone might recognize them.

"Since Monday's bombings, the FBI and our law enforcement partners have been working around the clock and are fully committed to investigating this matter to bring those responsible to justice," DesLauriers said. "Today, we are enlisting the public's help to identify the two suspects. . . . Suspect 1 is wearing a black hat. Suspect 2 is wearing a white hat."

As he talked, images of the two suspects were displayed. They were screenshots of videos showing the two men walking down Boylston Street on the day of the Boston Marathon.

"It is extremely important to contact us with any information regarding the identities of Suspect 1 and Suspect 2 and their locations," DesLauriers said. "We consider them to be armed and extremely dangerous."

Dias Kadyrbayev

Carriage Street, New Bedford, Massachusetts
Thursday, April 18, 2013, 8:43 p.m.

A little while after Dias Kadyrbayev returned home, his roommate, Azamat, left to go work out. Sometime after that, a friend texted Kadyrbayev to watch the news. He turned on the TV and was shocked at what he saw. The FBI did not know the names of the bombing suspects yet. But Kadyrbayev was confident that the images flashing on the screen were the Tsarnaev brothers. He could not believe that one of his best friends was a suspect in the Boston Marathon bombings.

He immediately texted Dzhokhar, "Yo bro."

"Wasup," Dzhokhar replied.

"Pick me up please," Kadyrbayev typed.

"Sorry man I'm in Boston," Dzhokhar texted.

Kadyrbayev had hoped to meet up with his friend.

He wanted to know if it was true; if the images that the FBI had posted were really of him and his brother.

Later he sent another text, "U saw the news?"

Y'ea bro I did," Dzhokhar replied.

Before their conversation ended, Dzhokhar said Kadyrbayev could take what he wanted from Dzhokhar's dorm room. Kadyrbayev was not sure if this meant his friend was leaving. He texted his roommate, asking to be picked up. As soon as Azamat returned home, the pair headed to Pine Dale Hall.

Dzhokhar was not in his room, and the door was locked. Other students milled about in the hallway. They had also seen the news. Some commented on the pictures that had been aired. Others noted that they also thought the picture looked a lot like Dzhokhar.

Kadyrbayev went in search of Dzhokhar's roommate. He found Dwinells in a study area. Dwinells had not heard the news yet, so it came as a shock to him. He told Kadyrbayev that Dzhokhar had left hours ago. Then he let Kadyrbayev and Azamat into the dorm room.

In Dzhokhar's half of the room, his friends spotted a black backpack. Inside were emptied fireworks.

The gunpowder had been taken out of them. There was also an empty jar of petroleum jelly.

"I think he used these to make the bombs," Kadyrbayev whispered.

Tamerlan and Dzhokhar Tsarnaev

Cambridge, Massachusetts
Thursday, April 18, 2013, 10:30 p.m.

Tamerlan and his brother stopped at the Massachusetts Institute of Technology (MIT) in Cambridge. They spotted a lone MIT police car in a parking lot. No one was around, so they sneaked up to the car.

As soon as they reached the patrol car, they jerked opened the door. Inside sat an officer.

They fired five shots.

Three bullets struck the officer, killing him.

Dzhokhar then reached into the car to take the officer's gun. But there was a lock on his holster. Dzhokhar could not open it.

So the Tsarnaev brothers fled the scene.

Officer Sean Collier was killed by the Tsarnaevs.

Dun "Danny" Meng

Third Street, Cambridge, Massachusetts
Thursday, April 18, 2013, 11:00 p.m.

Danny Meng pulled his black Mercedes Benz SUV to the curb. He had received a text that he wanted to answer. As he was typing, a knock startled him. There was a man in dark clothes standing outside his vehicle.

Meng rolled down the window to see what he wanted. That gave the man an opportunity to reach in and unlock the door. Then he jumped into the vehicle. Before Meng could react, the man pointed a gun straight at him.

Meng thought he was the victim of a robbery. He prepared to hand over what little cash he had. Instead, the man ordered Meng to drive him.

While on the road, the man asked Meng if he had heard about the bombing on Monday. Meng nodded.

"I did that," the man bragged. "And I just killed a policeman in Cambridge."

Meng's heart raced. He now knew he was involved in something much more serious than a carjacking. He began to fear for his life.

After a few miles, the man told Meng to pull over. As he did, a green Honda Civic stopped behind them. Another man got out. Meng did not know that the other man had been following them.

As Meng and the man with the gun switched seats, the other man loaded some boxes into the SUV.

Then they drove off. To Meng, the pair seemed unsure of where they were going, as if they did not have a plan. They wound their way aimlessly around Cambridge and Watertown. They spoke in Russian to each other, and at one point Meng picked out the word *Manhattan*.

Joseph Reynolds

Watertown Police Station, Watertown, Massachusetts
Thursday, April 18, 2013, 11:30 p.m.

Joseph Reynolds was one of the Watertown police officers preparing for duty late Thursday evening. He was about to begin a midnight to 8:00 a.m. shift. After roll call, the gathered officers heard some disturbing news. They were told that earlier in the evening an MIT officer had been shot and killed in neighboring Cambridge. This put them all on high alert, but no one connected the MIT shooting to Monday's bombing.

"Be on the lookout," their commanding officer told them. "And be safe."

Then Reynolds headed out on patrol. Other than the troubling report from MIT, it was a calm night.

Danny Meng made his escape from the Tsarnaev brothers at this Shell station in Cambridge, Massachusetts.

Dun "Danny" Meng

Cambridge, Massachusetts
Thursday, April 18, 2013, 11:55 p.m.

After nearly an hour of driving, the man at the wheel of Meng's SUV pulled into a Shell station in Cambridge because the car was almost out of gas. The station accepted only cash. While the other man ran inside to pay, the driver and Meng sat in the car.

Meng knew this was his chance to escape. The driver had set down the gun. Meng felt sure that if he did not run now, the men would kill him later. They had already set off deadly bombs at the marathon and claimed to have killed a police officer.

Danny Meng

Slowly, so the driver would not notice, Meng reached for the door. He held the door handle with one hand and his seatbelt with the other.

As the driver watched for his companion to return, Meng counted in his head, One. Two. Three. Four. Go! In one fluid motion, Meng unclipped his seatbelt and opened the door. Then he was running. Running as fast as he could. Running for his life.

Meng darted across the street to another gas station. He burst through the door screaming, "Please call 911! Please call 911!"

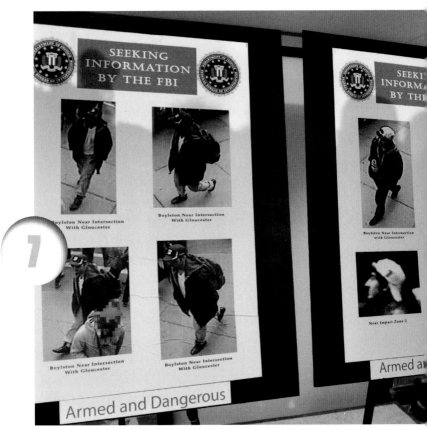

These posters were created to help the public identify the bombers.

SHOOTOUT ON LAUREL STREET

Joseph Reynolds

Joseph Reynolds's radio crackled to life. The dispatcher relayed news of a carjacking. He and his fellow officers on patrol were told to keep a lookout for a black SUV. The owner of the vehicle had said that two Middle Eastern–looking men had taken him hostage and stolen his car.

Because the SUV was equipped with a GPS system, the emergency dispatcher was able to ping the vehicle's location. The suspects were in Cambridge, not far from Reynolds's location. He headed in their direction.

Reynolds spotted the SUV parked next to a green Honda Civic on Dexter Avenue. He drove alongside the vehicles. For a second, he locked eyes with one of the suspects. And then he drove past them.

"I have the car!" he radioed in.

Reynolds was told not to engage and to wait for help. As he swung his car around, the suspects pulled away in the stolen SUV. Reynolds followed as they turned onto Laurel Street, while other officers sped toward their location. Then the black SUV stopped suddenly, and one of the suspects jumped out. He walked toward Reynolds's squad car and raised his arm. Shots rang out.

Reynolds ducked down and put his car in reverse. "Shots fired! Shots fired!" he shouted over the radio.

The shooter stood in the middle of the street and fired at Reynolds. When two more squad cars arrived, the shooter turned his gun on them. As the man exchanged gunshots with police officers, his companion jumped out of the SUV. He lit the fuse of an object that looked like a homemade pipe bomb. The man tossed the object down the street. It clunked on the pavement as it bounced toward the police officers. They ducked for cover. An explosion boomed, shaking the neighborhood.

Gunfire continued to ring out between the officers and the suspects. The bomber lit another

fuse and tossed the deadly object. The quiet
neighborhood of Watertown had become like a
war zone.

Jeffry Pugliese

Laurel Street, Watertown, Massachusetts
Friday, April 19, 2013, early morning hours

Sergeant Jeffry Pugliese of the Watertown Police
had recently gone off duty. He was driving home
when he heard reports of gunfire on his radio. He
quickly sped over to Laurel Street.

Once on the scene, Pugliese decided to flank the
suspects. He sneaked around the back of the houses
on Laurel Street, and then crept toward one suspect's
position.

When the suspect spotted Pugliese, he strutted
toward the officer and fired round after round.
Bullets whizzed by Pugliese. He fired back, and he
thought he hit the suspect. The man staggered, but
he kept marching toward Pugliese and firing.

Suddenly, the man's gun jammed. He glanced
down at it, not sure what to do, and then he tossed it

at Pugliese before turning to run. Pugliese saw this as his chance. He did not worry that the suspect might have explosives on him. He tackled the man from behind. Another officer jumped in to help subdue the suspect.

Joseph Reynolds

Laurel Street, Watertown, Massachusetts
Friday, April 19, 2013, early morning hours

Reynolds rushed over to help Pugliese and another officer. They had one suspect pinned in the middle of the street.

Just then, Reynolds heard an engine rev. He turned to see the black SUV barreling down the street toward them. The other suspect was behind the wheel of the vehicle.

"Sarge! Sarge!" Reynolds yelled. "He's coming!"

Reynolds watched as Pugliese grabbed the suspect by the belt and tried to drag him out of the street. The SUV raced by, barely missing Pugliese. But the suspect in the street was not so lucky. His companion in the SUV drove right over him, dragging him about 20 to 30 feet down the street.

Homes on Laurel Street were damaged during the battle between police and the Tsarnaevs.

When the SUV stopped moving, Reynolds ran over to help Pugliese handcuff the wounded suspect.

After the shootout someone shouted, "Officer down!"

Several officers had been injured, but Sergeant Richard Donohue was probably the worst off. He was losing a lot of blood from the gunshot wound to his leg. Reynolds grabbed his medic bag and ran over to help the other officers. They struggled to keep Donohue alive until an ambulance reached the scene.

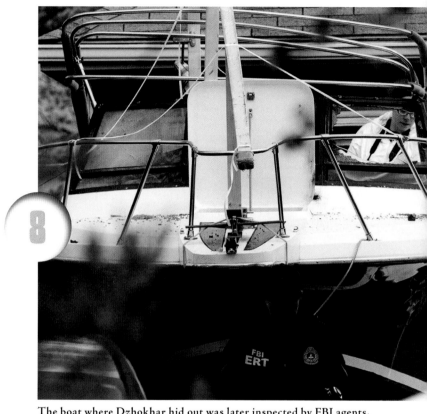

The boat where Dzhokhar hid out was later inspected by FBI agents.

IDENTIFY AND CAPTURE

Dzhokhar Tsarnaev

Franklin Street, Watertown,
Massachusetts
Friday, April 19, 2013, morning.

Dzhokhar had been struck by a police bullet while speeding away from the scene of the shootout. After being on the run for the past day, he was exhausted. Worse, he was now injured and bleeding from the shootout. He did not make it far in Meng's SUV before having to pull over.

After ditching the SUV, which was now known to the police, Dzhokhar crept through the quiet Watertown neighborhood along Franklin Street. As he ducked behind a house, he noticed a large boat with a plastic cover over the top of it. He crawled under the covering to hide inside the boat.

He did not know how many law enforcement officers were searching for him. There seemed to be no choice but to stay put. As he lay inside the boat, Dzhokhar scrawled a note on it—with his own blood. He wrote, "God has a plan for each person. Mine was to hide in his boat and shed some light on our actions . . ."

He tried to describe why he and his brother took the actions they did. "The U.S. Government is killing our innocent civilians but most of you already know that. As a M[uslim] I can't stand to see such evil go unpunished . . ." A few sentences later he wrote, "Now I don't like killing innocent people it is forbidden in Islam . . ." Then, after he wrote a few more words, exhaustion took over and he fell asleep.

Jeffrey Sallet

FBI Command Post, Boston, Massachusetts
Friday, April 19, 2013, 1:35 a.m.

Assistant Special Agent Jeffrey Sallet was on duty at the FBI command post in Boston when the news came through. Suspect 1, also known as

Black Hat, had been rushed to Beth Israel Deaconess Medical Center. He had been shot multiple times and run over. There was nothing that doctors could do to save him. He was declared dead at 1:35 a.m.

An FBI team went to the hospital. They took Black Hat's fingerprints with a Quick Capture Platform. The Quick Capture Platform immediately searched through the FBI database of fingerprints. It came back with a name: Tamerlan Tsarnaev.

From there, Sallet ran Tamerlan's name through the FBI's intelligence databases. They got a hit.

Back in 2011, Russian security forces had warned the FBI that Tamerlan might have ties to Chechen extremists. The FBI had even questioned Tamerlan about his activities, but at the time they found no evidence of terrorist activity.

Next, Sallet had FBI intelligence analysts search for Tamerlan's family connections. White Hat still hadn't been identified. To find him, Sallet thought it made sense to start with Tamerlan's family. A driver's license picture of Dzhokhar Tsarnaev popped up. A facial recognition expert compared it to images of White Hat. Sallet believed they had a match.

He was fairly certain that the two marathon bombing suspects were Tamerlan and Dzhokhar Tsarnaev.

David Henneberry

Franklin Street, Watertown, Massachusetts
Friday, April 19, 2013, 4:00 a.m.

David Henneberry and his wife received an automated call early Friday morning.

"Hello, this is Detective Connors with the Watertown Police Department," it began. "There is an active incident in Watertown right now. Chief

Police at first believed Dzhokhar was holed up in this house.

Deveau is advising all Watertown East End residents to remain in their homes."

After receiving the call, Henneberry peeked out his front window. He saw a group of heavily armed officers slowly walking down the street. He guessed they were a SWAT team. They were going house to house and knocking on doors. They checked sheds. They searched garages and questioned residents. They looked into cars and under porches. Henneberry also heard the whirl of helicopters hovering as they canvassed the area.

Governor Deval Patrick

Watertown, Massachusetts
Friday, April 19, 2013, morning

Early on the morning of April 19, Governor Deval Patrick learned about the shootout on Laurel Street. Not long after that, he was told that the SUV the suspect drove off in had been found in Watertown. There was blood in the vehicle, so officers believed that the suspect had been wounded during the shootout hours earlier. He could not have gotten far, injured and on foot.

To aid in the hunt for the suspect, Governor Patrick called for a lockdown of a 20-block radius around the area. Hours after he made this decision, he held a news conference to let the people of Massachusetts know what was happening.

". . . suspect 1 is dead. Suspect 2 is on the run," he reported. He also mentioned the officer who had been killed the night before and the officers who had been injured.

"There is a massive manhunt underway," he continued. ". . . we're asking people to shelter in place. In other words to stay indoors, with your doors locked, and not to open the door for anyone other than a properly identified law enforcement officer."

Cheryl Fiandaca

Twitter
Friday, April 19, 9:32 a.m., 2013

Cheryl Fiandaca's department posted a picture of Dzhokhar Tsarnaev on Twitter. Along with the picture was the message #WANTED: Updated photo of 19-year-old Dzhokhar Tsarnaev released. Suspect considered armed & dangerous.

Governor Deval Patrick

Watertown, Massachusetts
Friday, April 19, 2013, 6:00 p.m.

Putting part of the greater Boston area under lockdown had been a tough decision for Governor Patrick. He was asking thousands of people to stay home and shutting down the public transportation system. Businesses remained closed during the day, and even the Red Sox game at Fenway Park had been canceled that night. Not since 9/11 had a major city been shut down like this.

While Patrick had the authority to ask people to stay indoors, it was not something he could request of them indefinitely. People would need to get out to get food and go to work. Every hour Boston was shut down was costing the city and local businesses millions of dollars. Every hour the shelter-in-place request remained in effect,

Governor Deval Patrick held several news conferences during the search for the Boston Marathon bombers.

more and more people would question his decision. He also knew that if it remained in effect for too long, he might get a call from the federal government asking him to defend his request. So shortly after 6:00 p.m. Governor Patrick held a news conference and announced that he was lifting the stay-indoors request.

David Henneberry

Franklin Street, Watertown, Massachusetts
Friday, April 19, 2013, night

Shortly after Governor Patrick announced that the stay-indoors request was lifted, Henneberry stepped out the back door. It was nice to get outside after being stuck in the house all day. As he glanced around his yard, he noticed some of the shrink wrap around his boat had come loose. He grabbed a ladder and climbed up to clamp it down.

That is when he saw the blood. It was smeared on the side of the boat. Peeking under the plastic, he spotted a wounded man lying on the bottom of the boat. The man was perfectly still.

Henneberry hurriedly climbed down the ladder and rushed inside. He told his wife that he needed to call 9-1-1.

William Evans

Superintendent Evans was on duty. He happened to be near Henneberry's house when dispatch radioed about a suspicious character found there. He was one of the first officers on the scene. He immediately took charge as more and more squad cars swooped in with sirens wailing. Law enforcement personnel took up positions around the boat where the suspect was thought to be hiding. Some officers were on the ground, ducking behind cars and houses. Snipers got up on rooftops. A state police helicopter hovered overhead. It had an infrared camera that could detect any movement under the plastic wrap. Anyone hiding in that boat was not going to escape. Evans just hoped they could arrest him alive. But for them to do that, the suspect needed to be forced out of the boat.

Evans also called in a tactical team. He worried

that the suspect might be armed with more bombs, or possibly even be wearing an explosive vest. Evans did not want anyone moving in until he knew it was safe to do so.

The tactical team arrived and prepared to use flash bangs. These non-deadly grenades would give off a bright light and a thunderous bang. Evans hoped they would drive the suspect out from his hiding spot. The team exploded one just above the boat. Bang! The helicopter team continued keeping watch from above with their infrared camera. They reported no movement.

The tactical officers fired a second flash bang. The camera operator reported movement. Evans had the tactical team prepare to move in.

Then the suspect began to crawl out of the boat. The situation was tense. No one knew what he might do. Tactical officers rushed in and handcuffed the suspect. The manhunt was over.

After police captured Dzhokhar Tsarnaev, they sent him to a hospital to have his wounds treated.

Cheryl Fiandaca

Twitter
Friday, April 19, 2013, 8:58 p.m.

Not long after Dzhokhar's capture, Fiandaca's department tweeted: "CAPTURED!!! The hunt is over. The search is done. The terror is over. And justice has won. Suspect in custody."

EPILOGUE

On April 25, 10 days after the marathon bombing, David McGillivray once again laced up his running shoes. He arrived in Hopkinton around 8:30 a.m. It was time for him to run the Boston Marathon's course, to add to his 40-year streak. But he was not the only one whose running of the Boston Marathon had been interrupted at 2:49 p.m. on April 15.

A month later, on May 25, about 3,000 runners gathered to run the final mile of the course. Many of them had been injured, and others had been prevented from finishing the race. "Boston Strong" became the rallying cry of Boston and its residents after the bombing. The people running on May 25 were prime examples of what those words meant. They were determined to remain resilient and not let the tragedy of the bombings keep them down.

The bombings and the events following them left more than 250 people injured and four people dead. Eight-year old Martin Richard was with his parents, sister, and brother in front of Marathon

Dzhokhar Tsarnaev appeared in court flanked by his defense attorneys to stand trial for his role in the deaths of four and wounding of 250 others.

Sports when the first bomb went off. His sister lost a leg, his mom an eye, his dad received severe burns, but shrapnel from the bomb killed Martin. Lingzi Lu was with a friend near the Forum restaurant when the second bomb exploded. She was thrown to the ground and injured by shrapnel. When Dr. Natalie Stavas rushed in to help people, she performed CPR on Lu. But Lu's injuries were too severe, and she died before reaching the hospital. Krystle Campbell was also near the Forum. She had gone with a friend to take pictures of the Boston Marathon and died as a result of the second explosion. However, the quick action of medical staff and first responders helped prevent more deaths.

Sean Collier was the fourth person killed by the Tsarnaevs. He was the MIT campus police officer who was shot April 18 as they were fleeing. It is unclear which of the Tsarnaevs shot Collier. During his trial Dzhokhar claimed that his brother had killed the officer.

Almost two years after Dzhokhar Tsarnaev's capture, he was found guilty on 30 federal counts, which included the murder of Collier and plotting to use a weapon of mass destruction. On June 24, 2015, he received a death sentence. The outcome of the trial was another step in Boston's healing after the bombing. Dzhokhar is currently being held in a maximum-security prison in Florence, Colorado, while his sentence is under appeal.

There is still a lot of mystery surrounding the Tsarnaev brothers' motivations and actions leading up to the bombing. During his trial, Dzhokhar revealed few details, and now, while his sentence is under appeal, Dzhokhar has not been allowed to talk to the media. It is unclear if the full details surrounding the Tsarnaevs' actions will ever be known.

The fates of some of the others are known:

Within 24 hours of Dzhokhar's capture, roommates Dias Kadyrbayev and Azamat Tazhayakov were arrested at the apartment they rented in New Bedford, Massachusetts. A couple of days earlier, while in their friend's dorm room,

Dias Kadyrbayev (left) and Azamat Tazhayakov were tried and convicted for their role in covering up Dzhokhar's role in the bombing.

they had taken the backpack they had found with the emptied fireworks and jar of Vaseline. Along with that, they took their friend's laptop computer, a thumb drive, and other items they thought might incriminate their friend. They thought they were protecting their friend, whom they suspected was just following his big brother's lead. Then Kadyrbayev and Tazhayakov threw everything they had taken into a dumpster. For their actions, they were charged with obstruction of justice, found guilty, and served jail time.

Shortly after her husband's death, Katherine Russell left Boston with her daughter, Zahara, to stay with her parents in North Kingston, Rhode Island. FBI agents visited her several times there to ask about events surrounding the Boston Marathon bombing. They also wanted to know whether Tamerlan had planned any other bombings. Russell denied any knowledge of her husband's actions and plans. She has never been charged with any wrongdoing regarding the bombings.

Carlos Arredondo and Jeff Bauman met again during the Celebrity Mile of the Runners World

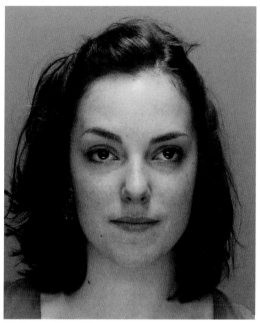
Katherine Russell

Classic held in Andover, Massachusetts, in 2016.
Arredondo, who had pushed Bauman to safety after
the 2013 Boston Marathon bombing, was now in
a wheelchair himself after surgery. For Bauman, it
was the first time he had been able to take part in an
athletic event since having both of his legs amputated
from just above the knees. He was slowly moving
on prosthetic legs, and with about 100 yards left, he
stepped behind Arredondo to push him toward the
finish line.

A crowd of other runners kept pace with Bauman and Arredondo. As the pair crossed the finish line, a loud cheer went out. They were then given medals for participating and completing the run. Being able to complete a mile run was a huge victory for Bauman. A year later, a movie would come out that told of Bauman's life, how he lost his legs during the Boston bombing, and his struggles to cope with his injuries. It was based on a memoir he wrote titled *Stronger*.

President Barack Obama honored Natalie Stavas for her bravery, *Bostonian* magazine named her one of "Boston's Best" when she and several others appeared on its cover, and the *Boston Globe* named her 2013's Bostonian of the Year. While she continues to work in health care, she has also become a motivational speaker. During her talks she tells the story of how she chose to run toward the danger after the bombs went off at the marathon.

"You always have two directions," she says. "You can run towards that which people say you shouldn't, or you can run the other way."

The 118th running of the Boston Marathon was held on April 21, 2014. The bombing a year earlier did not prevent the city from holding its annual event. Boston truly remained strong—as did those who experienced the bombing.

Today the Boston Marathon is still one of the most prestigious races in the world. Security measures on Marathon Mondays have since been heightened. Bags such as backpacks are no longer permitted in areas where there are large crowds. The number of police officers on hand has risen. Some officers are stationed on rooftops to keep an eye on buildings along the route while thousands more undercover officers mingle within crowds on the ground. More bomb- and chemical-sniffing dogs than in the past are on hand with K-9 units. Along with helicopters, surveillance drones are also deployed.

The tragedy has not dampened people's excitement about the event. Marathon Mondays are still festive. Thousands of people run in the race, and hundreds of thousands of spectators cheer them on to the finish line.

TIMELINE

APRIL 15, 9:00 A.M., 2013—The 117th running of the Boston Marathon gets under way.

APRIL 15, 10:20 A.M., 2013—Wave two, with Dr. Natalie Stavas and her father, starts the race.

APRIL 15, 2:37 P.M., 2013—Video footage shows that the Tsarnaev brothers were on Boylston Street.

APRIL 15, 2:49 P.M., 2013—A bomb explodes near the Boston Marathon's finish line. Moments later, a second explosion occurs just a block away. Three people are killed and more than 250 are injured.

APRIL 15, 6:10 P.M., 2013—President Barack Obama goes on National TV to address events of the Boston Marathon bombing.

APRIL 16, 2013—The FBI team discovers the lid to one of the pressure cookers the Tsarnaev brothers used to make their bombs.

APRIL 18, 5:20 P.M., 2013—FBI investigators release photos of two suspects. They ask for help from the public in identifying the two men.

April 18, 10:30 p.m., 2013—The Tsarnaev brothers shoot a police officer and steal a vehicle.

April 19, 1:35 am, 2013—Tamerlan is pronounced dead after being shot and then run over by an SUV driven by his brother.

April 19, 8:58 p.m., 2013—The Boston Police Department announces that Dzhokhar has been captured.

April 8, 2015—Dzhokhar is found guilty of 30 federal counts against him.

June 24, 2015—Dzhokhar is formally sentenced to death; to date, he is being held at a maximum-security prison in Florence, Colorado, while his case is under appeal.

GLOSSARY

analyst (an-uh-LYST)—a person who studies information, such as the evidence at a crime scene

amputate (AM-pyuh-tayt)—to remove or cut off

database (DAY-tuh-bays)—a large collection of data that is stored electronically

elite (i-LEET)—top performer, best of the best

forensic (FUH-REN-SIK)—having to do with searching for scientific knowledge to solve crimes

mobility-impaired (mo-BIL-i-te im-PAIRD)—having some sort of limitations or needing assistance, such as crutches or an artificial limb, to walk

prosthetic (PROSS-THET-IK)—an artificial limb

resilient (ri-ZIL-yent)—able to withstand difficult situations

shrapnel (SHRAP-NUHL)—pieces of bomb fragments that fly out from an explosion

spectator (SPEK-tay-tur)—one who watches an event

suspect (SUHSS-pekt)—a person thought to have committed a crime

SWAT Team (SWAHT TEEM)—Special Weapons and Tactics Team

CRITICAL THINKING QUESTIONS

1. When Dzhokhar Tsarnaev's college friends realized that Dzhokhar had committed a terrorist act, their response was to hide evidence that might convict him. What would you do if you realized a close friend or family member had committed a crime? Turn him or her in, or protect the person? Explain your choice.

2. The Boston Marathon bombing resulted in increased security at all future marathons, but with 30,000 runners, there's still a chance of danger. Do you think it was a good idea to continue running the marathons every year? Why or why not?

3. Dzhokhar Tsarnaev was sentenced to death for his crimes. Dzhokhar Tsarnaev was 19 years old when he and his brother set off the fatal bombs. Do you believe the death penalty should be enforced for acts committed by a teenager? Why or why not?

INTERNET SITES

Use FactHound to find Internet sites related to this book.

Visit *www.facthound.com*

Just type in 9781543541960 and go.

FURTHER READING

Baldino, Greg. *Investigating the Boston Marathon Bombings*. New York: Rosen Publishing Group, 2018.

Challen, Paul. *Surviving the Boston Marathon Bombing*. New York: Rosen Publishing, 2016.

Williams, Heather. *2013 Boston Marathon*. Ann Arbor, MI: Cherry Lake Publishing, 2019.

SELECTED BIBLIOGRAPHY

Bauman, Jeff, and Brett Witter. *Stronger*. New York: Grand Central Publishing, 2014.

Clerici, Paul C. *Boston Marathon History by the Mile*. Charleston, SC: The History Press, 2014.

Gessen, Masha. *Brothers: The Road to an America Tragedy*. New York: Riverhead Books, 2015.

INDEX

Arredondo, Carlos, 34–36, 102–104

Bauman, Jeff, 27, 33–34, 57–58, 67, 102–104
Black Hat, 62, 69, 87
bombs, 9, 26, 27, 29, 37, 39–40, 44, 53, 59, 61, 62, 63–64, 72, 80, 81, 106

cameras, 46, 59–60, 60–63
Campbell, Krystle, 99–100
casualties, 30–31, 33–34, 35–36, 48–49, 72, 83, 87, 90, 98–100, 103, 106, 107
Collier, Sean, 72, 100

Davis, Edward, 39, 46
DesLauriers, Richard, 44–46, 53–54, 56, 58–60, 63–64, 68–70
Donohue, Richard, 83
Dwinells, Andrew, 65, 71

Evans, William, 21–23, 38–40, 94–95
evidence, 44–46, 53–54, 56, 59

FBI, 44, 45, 49, 53, 58, 60, 67, 69, 70, 71, 86, 87, 102, 106
Fiandaca, Cheryl, 46, 48, 90–91, 97

Henneberry, David, 88–89, 93, 94
Hurley, Erin, 27

Kadyrbayev, Dias, 70–72, 101–102

Lu, Lingzi, 99

Massachusetts Institute of Technology (MIT), 72, 75, 100
McGillivray, David, 10–13, 37–38, 98
Meng, Dun "Danny," 73–75, 76–77
Menino, Thomas, Sr., 16–19, 40–41, 49, 55–56
Mueller, Robert, 49

Obama, Barack, 49–51, 104, 106

Patrick, Deval, 17, 44, 49, 54–55, 89–90, 91–92

Pugliese, Jeffry, 81–82, 83

Reynolds, Joseph, 75, 79–81, 82–83
Richard, Martin, 61, 98–99
Russell, Katherine, 24, 102

Sallet, Jeffrey, 86–88
Stavas, Joseph, 14, 15–16, 28–29
Stavas, Natalie, 13–16, 28–31, 99, 104, 106
Swindon, Kevin, 60–63

Tazhayakov, Azamat, 57, 68, 70, 71, 101–102
Tercetti, Gilberto, 56–57
Tsarnaev, Dzhokhar, 9, 23, 24, 25–26, 43–44, 48–49, 56–57, 65, 67–68, 70–71, 72, 85–86, 87–88, 90–91, 93—95, 97, 100–101, 106, 107
Tsarnaev, Tamerlan, 9, 23–25, 43–44, 57, 70, 71, 72, 87—88, 102, 106, 107
Tsarnaev, Zahara, 24, 102

White Hat, 62, 69, 87–88

ABOUT THE AUTHOR

Blake Hoena grew up on a farm in central Wisconsin. He moved to Minnesota to pursue an MFA in creative writing at Minnesota State University, Mankato. He has written more than 100 books for children, from graphic novels to picture books. Blake is also an avid runner and mountain biker. He lives in St. Paul with his two hounds, Ty and Stitch.